You Knew Me Then,

BUT YOU SEE ME NOW!

Forgiveness: giving up the hope that the past could have been any other way.

FELICIA PORTWINE

Book Cover Design: Prize Publishing House

Printed by: Prize Publishing House, LLC in the United States of America.

First printing edition 2021.

Prize Publishing House

P.O. Box 9856, Chesapeake, VA 23321

www.PrizePublishingHouse.com

Library of Congress Control Number: 2021914939

ISBN (Paperback): 978-1-7374791-3-0

ISBN (E-Book): 978-1-7374791-4-7

PREFACE

When people (women) do not deal with their unresolved issues, those issues in return become their reality! Muse on that for a moment. The definition of the word issue is: "a matter that is in dispute between two or more parties" ("Issue"). I'm of the belief that you are disputing with reality and yourself. If the problem is not dealt with or discussed eventually, in the end, it becomes a long-lasting reality. **Reality**: the world or the state of things as they actually exist, **instead of an idealistic or notional idea of them**. In other words, unresolved issues become part of who we are.

People (women) often move around in this world, holding on to hurts, pains, and emotional damages of the past. Holding on to the past appears better than intentionally letting go, in the natural sense, as if it never existed. However, in the spiritual sense, letting go simply means **"YES"** it existed but choosing not to let it define who you are. Like you, I choose not to let negative experiences control me or become a part of who I am. They will not be my reality! This book will reveal how letting go of the past will put you on track to your God-given destiny. Letting go of past hurts and pains doesn't weaken you but allows you to become the person (woman) you were meant to be. My prayer is that God will use this book to show you the difference between living in the past and walking in your purpose. Know that it was never about you! Release and trust the process.

DEDICATION

I would like to take this opportunity first to thank God, who is the author and finisher of my faith. To my husband, thank you for loving me through the good, the bad, and the ugly. To my daughters, thanks for understanding and for always encouraging me to be the best version of myself. Because of you, I am writing this book to encourage all the people (women) who have been struggling with forgiveness and resentment. To my friends (you know who you are), thanks for listening to my story over and over and over again. With gratitude, I say thanks for all your love, hugs, listening ears, and shoulders that I have leaned and cried on so many times. I love you.

-Fe

TABLE OF CONTENTS

INTRODUCTION

When it comes to forgiveness, if you first seek to understand, then you can forgive. Life's hurts, disappointments, and failures are what define our very existence and who we ultimately become. We can choose to stay there or move forward. Each step we take to move into forgiveness is a step towards owning our past. If we are bold enough to say that the past is the past, then we, in turn, must give in to the fact that forgiveness is inevitable. Forgiveness does not take away what happened; it says I will not allow it to control me. If we could turn back the hands of time, each of us would not choose whatever it was that caused the hurt or the pain. However, if we took a closer look at our lives, we could simply put it this way: I am who I am today because of what hurt me.

This book will reveal some areas in which we must come to terms with who we really are. We must know that what happened in the past was never about us. It's left up to us to take back the control that has controlled us far too long. Remember: forgiveness is not for the accuser or abuser but for you. Many say that hurting people generally hurt others, but have you ever thought of it this way? If a person does not know they are hurt, they may never know that they are hurting others. We must learn to trust that this is a part of the process. Healing must come in order for us to move into the things God has called us to. We are overcomers! I am not saying it will be easy, but it is doable. Here is a nugget, courtesy of my counselor, "You will never know how strong you are until you have to forgive someone who was not sorry or accept an apology you may never receive." My prayer is that this book will begin the healing process for some and remind others not to allow forgiveness to be the end of their story but rather the beginning to life.

CHAPTER 1

I Have to Heal in Order to Forgive

When we do not deal with our unresolved issues,
they become our reality.

We become so consumed with the pain of our past that it clouds our future. Holding on to that hurt becomes our identity and who we say we are. We must begin to understand that our past does not define our being, nor does it define our existence. For example, let's look at the word forgiveness. Forgiveness is the intentional and voluntary process by which a person undergoes a change in feelings and attitudes regarding an offense and overcomes negative emotions such as resentment and vengeance. It is imperative to understand forgiveness is necessary to move into our future and, ultimately, our destiny. Forgiveness is never for the accuser but the victim (YOU) regardless of how justified you are. Forgiveness doesn't always mean reconciliation; one doesn't have to return to the same relationship or accept the same behaviors of the offender. Again, forgiveness is not for the offender. Let's just sum the word forgiveness.

Forgiveness is knowing that the past could not have been any different. At the age of six, I became the victim of molestation. This continued for about 12 years. At the age of 18, my past would become my reality, or so I thought. Everything that happened to me would come to light. Just let me say, I come from a home where what happened there stayed there. The very moment things began to take a turn, everything would become my fault. Yes, you are reading this right. Everything was my fault. I carried this pain, hurt, and unbearable burden for over 30 years. This was who I was. When you are told that everything happened because of you, that is what you believe. I was only 18!

I had just graduated from high school and was about to leave home for the first time. The very person I thought would protect me was the one who denied me: my mother. She did not understand or know how that would affect me or who I would become. She took my accuser's side! You will understand this as you continue to read. I remember the evening this all took place; it turned my world upside down. Feeling a sense of guilt and embarrassment, I remember asking my mother if she would not tell my dad and just allow me to leave home and not return. Wow, what a request! Without saying a word, I knew that her silence gave consent.

The next morning I found myself boarding a bus with a great sense of disbelief and fear. I was able to stay with other (distant) family members who at the time had no idea of the circumstances. I am not proud of the fact that I lied to have a place to lay my head. After about two weeks, I decided to contact my mother to ask if I could come back home as things did not go as planned. She reluctantly agreed, and so I returned. Upon my return, I could still see the hurt in her eyes; she sat me down to discuss everything that had happened and inform me that she had told my dad. I thought to myself, *this is it for me*. She began telling me how disappointed she was with me and my actions as if it were my fault. She went on to say some other hurtful things, which I now understand because hurting people hurt others. She went on to say that I owed the accuser and his wife (yes, he and his wife) an apology. By the way, the accuser was an uncle. Now you understand the story.

Wanting to please my mother, I felt there were no other options. I told her how sorry I was and that I would never hurt her again. Doing what she demanded, I asked for forgiveness from my uncle and aunt. Let me clarify: these were not blood relatives. Small country towns tend to make everybody relatives. As the evening went on, my dad arrived home. While I was waiting in my room for him to enter, I begin to pray. You see, I was raised in the church and had accepted Jesus as my Lord and Savior at the age of twelve. knew how to pray. As my dad entered, my heart sank in knowing what would happen next.

Like my mother, he too sat me down and reiterated that this was entirely my fault, how disappointed he was, and that if he ever caught me at their (my uncle's) house again, he would have me (ME!) locked up. You would have to know my dad to understand the impact of this conversation. However, I told him I understood, and I would never enter their home again. Thinking this was the end of the conversation, I found myself being slapped multiple times in the face.

That night while lying in bed is what I call the first night of the rest of my life. Weeks had passed, and there were no real interactions or conversations leading up to my going away to college. The time had come for me to leave. In September of 1984, I left home, and nothing was ever the same again. Months had passed and all I could do was replay my mother's words, trying to make some sense of it all. I never had the chance to tell her that not only was I being molested by my uncle, but a cousin was also molesting me. I mean, how could I tell her; would she even believe me, or would she just deny me again? I never mentioned it, and to this day, she has no idea or knowledge of those occurrences.

It would take me over three decades to begin my walk into forgiveness and release the resentment that came along with holding on to my past. To heal, first, YOU must make a conscious decision to FORGIVE. Honestly, the best feeling ever is realizing you're not angry or bitter anymore about something you thought you would never recover from or get over.

Minister Andy Stanley states:

"In the shadow of my hurt, forgiveness feels like a decision to reward my enemy. But in the shadow of the cross, forgiveness is merely a gift from one undeserving soul to another. Forgiveness is the gift that ensures my freedom from the prison of bitterness and resentment." (Stanley, 2012)

> *"Even as the Lord has freely forgiven you, so must you also forgive" (Colossians 3:13, AMP).*

CHAPTER 2

It's Never About You!

You can't wait for an apology to receive your closure.

I often find myself asking, *God, why me*? Was I not good enough? Why did this have to happen to me? Anger is a punishment you give yourself for someone else's mistake. That was my place in life. After three decades of holding on to this horrific and unbearable pain, I began seeking help from not one, not two, not three, but four different counselors. Like I stated in the previous chapter, I accepted Jesus at the age of twelve and knew what the Word of God said about forgiving. However, sometimes it is easier said than done. As time went on, I thought I had forgiven, but somehow it kept creeping back into my life. Keep in mind that forgiveness is not for the other person. It is for you! It is the process of remembering without anger. It frees up your mind and heals your body. Forgiveness opens up a pathway to a new place of peace where you can keep moving despite what happened to you. Perhaps it was hard for me because I still came in contact with my uncle during family gatherings.

Skipping to two years later, after leaving home, I got married. Guess who performed the ceremony? Yes! You may be wondering "why," but it was because my mother insisted. Remember me making the promise to my mother never to hurt her again? Well, this is what my life had become as I lived to keep that promise. At the time, my soon-to-be husband had no clue of the molestation (of course not); he would not find out until a few years later. I felt my life was spiraling out of control. You see, words are powerful! When I spoke the words "I will never hurt you again" to my mother, this was the seed that was planted and would begin to grow. Yes, I was in church hearing the Word, reading the Word, and praying, but I could not seem to shake the demons that were torturing my mind. Seeking help and trying to forgive became a constant for me, a relentless battle.

It was not until 30 years later that I would find my relief. My husband's job had moved us to Atlanta, and I was working in the local school district. It was what seemed to be a typical day, one year to date of my dad's passing. The school day had ended, and school had been dismissed. A voice came over the radio stating that we had a student that had not been picked up, so the parent needed to be notified. I looked up the number and phoned the parent. This was the beginning of a ripple effect of how out of control my emotions really were, again, 30 years later. Needless to say, after a brief confrontation with the parent, I found myself sitting in the office of my third counselor. Now, what was I to do? She began talking, and all I could do was cry. This went on for weeks. Talk about a whirlwind. This again, Lord? Are you serious? Lord, you know I have forgiven not only my mom and dad but also my uncle and aunt. After about the third or fourth visit with the counselor, she suggested that I begin to write. My previous counselors had suggested the same thing, and as I told them, "Writing makes it a reality." So, I refused to put it on paper for the time being.

After thinking about this for a few weeks, I reluctantly began to write. By the way, this brings me to writing this book. Through writing, I soon realized that, while I had forgiven, I was still holding on to resentment. Forgiveness and resentment are two different things. I resented the fact that my mother had not protected me but had sided with them. THEM! Resentment is accepting something that was so very wrong, knowing it wasn't your fault. That's my version. No way Lord, no!! You mean I was still holding onto something? I was in church and reading and quoting scriptures, yet struggling. How many of you can identify? It is possible to forgive and still resent someone or something at the same time. What an eye-opener. Do not spend your energy wrestling over the past. Your pain will make you bitter or better. The choice is yours.

As I began to dig a little deeper and write more and more, it was like peeling away layers and layers of emotional pain and hurt.

Side note: most victims of molestation never think about the act but all the emotions that are attached to the act.

For the first time, I could see the light at the end of the tunnel. Praise God! Then one day, I was praying and crying out to God; He hears, and He answers prayers. To my amazement, the Lord asked: "Have you ever thought about your mother's past (her life)? It's not about you, and it never was."

This statement shook me to the very core of my being. What do you mean it was never about me? Remember the statement in chapter one: when we do not deal with our unresolved issues, it becomes our reality. My mother, whom I never stopped loving or respecting, has never dealt with her unresolved issues, and they became her reality. I had to take a step back and ask God to show me the entire picture. Then I began to remember some of the things I had overheard as a child regarding my mother's childhood. It all became clear; this is how our unresolved issues become our reality! So, without her knowing, her past was her reality. Enough said, right? Disclaimer: This does not mean my mother was, nor is she, a bad person. The fact is that she never dealt with the emotional pains and hurts of her past and unresolved issues. I also want to iterate that before my dad passed, I had made peace with him.

Note to self: I can't wait for someone to say "I'm sorry" to receive my closure. You must not allow life to stop.

CHAPTER 3

God, I Don't Understand But I Know You Have a Plan

Life is not about the bruises; it is about collecting the scars to prove you showed up!

The Lord states in Jeremiah 29:11: "For I know the thoughts that I think towards you, saith the Lord, thoughts of peace, and not of evil, to give you an expected end" (KJV).

Even though I had to endure this pain and trauma as a child, I now know that I am who I am because of what I endured. Life did not just stop at the devastation of being molested. At the age of 16, I became pregnant (sometimes, being molested causes one to become promiscuous). I am not making excuses or justifying *my* actions. The answer to your question is no; I did not get pregnant by my uncle. This happened two years before I would disclose the molestation. Unfortunately, even though I was being molested, I was still searching for love or what I thought was love. Perhaps this is what led to my mother's actions

12

regarding finding out about the molestation. I am sure this was hard for her to take in. Please understand that I am not justifying my mom's actions or reactions to dealing with this because I was still a child, her child!

I carried the baby for eight months only to deliver a stillborn little girl. This was devastating to a young girl who had never even heard the word stillborn. I had no time to process all of this or understand the dynamics of its seriousness and all the mental and emotional baggage that would come along with it. To my amazement, before I could leave the hospital, my dad had already made arrangements to have the baby buried. I have no idea where she is buried to this day. After being released two days later, I came home never to mention or discuss this devastating yet horrific ordeal again. I was left to figure it all out, pick up the pieces and move on. This was August 7th (the birth date of my baby girl), just a few weeks before school would start.

The first day of school hit the hardest for me. As I walked into the gym, I was approached by some of my classmates, who obviously had not heard the news regarding my delivery. They were excited to find out the name, sex, and arrival of the baby. I stood there for a moment, still trying to process the whole tribulation alone! Slowly, I opened my mouth and uttered the words, "S*he didn't live*." They, of course, were apologetic and filled with emotion as the news saddened them. The pep rally began, and I sat with my face turned away as the tears fell down my face; I do not remember anything that happened after that. There were times I thought it was all a dream. So, God, You mean all of this was just a part of the plan? You mean I had to go through this to get to where You are taking me? Now that I look back on my life and know what I know today, I am behooved at the hand of God and His complexity of divine order, even in the midst of what I see and what I feel to be disorderly. Although I endured the pain of losing a child, thank God for His mercy and grace that eventually extended me the opportunity and blessing of (in marriage) birthing two beautiful amazing, and talented daughters. He gave me double.

The Lord gives beauty for ashes: "To appoint unto them that mourn in Zion, to give unto them beauty for ashes, the oil of joy for mourning, the garment of praise for the spirit of heaviness; that they might be called trees of righteousness, the planting of the Lord, that he might be glorified" (Isaiah 61:3, KJV).

CHAPTER 4

It's About the Process, Not the Problem

Do not despise the process.

In the midst of my process, I had to learn how to be in love with the person who had been through so much: *me*. Thank God that I am still standing and still here. I had to love myself and stop hating the experiences that shaped me. As stated earlier, even though I had a rough childhood, it was all a part of the process. The past is a place of reference, not a place of residence. As unimaginable as this sounds, I now find myself understanding the hand of God. You see, God had His hands on me even when I was enduring such tragedy, such hurt, and such pain. There were many times I thought God had left me or forgotten me, but He was waiting for me to realize who I was in Him. The enemy tried to destroy me but to no avail. But GOD! I am not saying that I do not struggle with the memories; I am still human.

The enemy will always try to keep your past at the forefront of your mind. This is why we must do as God's Word directs and be in a constant state of practicing what 2 Corinthians 10:5 states: "Casting down imaginations, and every high thing that exalted itself against the knowledge of God, and bringing into captivity every thought to the obedience of Christ" (KJV). You can forgive and still have the memories of life's indecencies. Let's take a look at the word process: a natural or involuntary series of changes. Changes, yes, changes, are inevitable and will be a constant from the time you are born. The key to navigating change well is managing your thoughts and casting down whatever does not line up with the Word of God. Again, I am not giving glory to what I went through as a child, but now that I have grown into the woman that I am, I am able to understand the hand of God.

Someone once said, "God is the great chess player" (anonymous). I have found it to be a true statement in many cases. What I went through wasn't good for me, but it has and is working for my good. Romans 8:28 states: "And we know that all things work together for good to them that love God, to them that are called according to his purpose" (KJV). You see, although my beginning was dark and blurred, my ending has a light at the end of the tunnel. You may recall my earlier statement that my mother is not a bad person, just a person with unresolved issues. Well, there is some good to the story. Amid her shortcomings, I learned how to be a wife and a mother. I learned how to manage money (she always had good credit). She taught me how to keep a house, wash clothes, and prepare food. All of this was part of the plan, even when I did not see it.

I am learning how to unleash the past and consciously choose to focus on the process and not the problem. Forgiveness is knowing that the past could not have been any different. You can never learn what God is trying to teach you until you get to a place where people (especially negative voices from your past) can no longer reach you. My plea to you is not to despise the process. Begin to deny the past to control your future. God has a plan, but you have to go through the problem to understand the process and the plan. God's Word reveals this truth: "For I know the thoughts that I think toward you, saith the Lord, thoughts of peace, and not of evil, to give you an expected end." (Jeremiah 29:11, KJV). I know I have quoted this scripture in the previous chapter, but I am trying to get you to understand that our past cannot define or dictate who we are or who we will become unless we allow it to. An end can only be achieved by allowing the process to work. Life is more than holding on to the past. We have to move on to be a better us.

I charge you with this: choose to forgive and let go of resentment so that you can move into your future, your destiny, and your purpose. Learn to accept the things you cannot change and change the things you can, starting with your thought process. Again, do not focus on the problem, but look beyond life's tragedies and begin to allow God to take you through the process.

CHAPTER 5

Trust the Process

You are tougher than the test!

Philippians 1:6 encourages us with this: "Being confident of this very thing, that He which hath begun a good work in you will perform it until the day of Jesus Christ" (KJV). I begin this chapter with that scripture because no matter how your beginning begins, you still have a purpose and destiny to look forward to. Your future is far greater than your past. There's something about the woman who overcomes everything that is meant to destroy her. Trusting the process is a hard task, especially when it seems like the odds are stacked against you from your very existence. We have to trust God even when we do not understand the plan. When you begin to look at the root or background of a person, then you start to understand their motives and behaviors. When you understand, then you can begin to travel the road to forgiveness. The road might begin rocky, but the end can be smooth-paved. Because of my mother's childhood and a portion of her adulthood, she became bitter. She lowered her self-esteem just to please other people. Again, this does not make my mom a bad person; these are things she just did not know had resolved to be her reality. It was who she had allowed herself to become.

Looking at the big picture that surrounded my past, one might predict that my life would mimic her life, but not according to Philippians 1:6. What God has for your life, no matter how it presently looks, He will bring to fulfillment and completion. Let me just say that forgiveness is not forgetting; it is simply letting go. Trusting the process is not always easy, although it is doable. Let me repeat that statement: *trusting the process is not always easy, although it is doable*. The greater the pain, the greater the process or purpose! Just know you are tougher than you think. You are tougher than the test! Take a step back and take a long look at your life.

First and foremost, you are still here! How many times have you wanted to give up and throw in the towel? For me, it was and sometimes still is a daily battle. There is an old cliché that states it is easier said than done. You can choose not to allow the past to control you; however, the past is still the past. No, I am not contradicting myself; it's still a choice to let go and forgive.

It takes a strong person to forgive and begin trusting the process. Of course, I wish I didn't have to endure such pain and hurt, but it was a part of my process. We all have a purpose and a destiny, but it's the process that gets us to our destination. Remember, the process is a series of changes. Who likes change? Almost no one! However, to reach the destination, change will and has to take place. Sometimes it seems easier to hold on to the past because that's what is familiar or comfortable. That is a hard statement, but a true statement. Not forgiving is an entrapment that keeps you locked in and ultimately stops progress. Forgiveness doesn't come easy, but not forgiving someone is to elevate them to be the most influential person in your life. You essentially give them the power over your thoughts, emotions, and the path your life will eventually take. It has taken me over 30 years to get to this place I am in, and I now realize that I am tougher than I thought! I am still learning to trust the process. Trusting the process covers everything in life.

I am thankful to my husband and my children for loving me through this process. They never gave up on me, and for that, I am grateful. Their words to me have always been, "You are tougher than you think!"

CHAPTER 6

Looking Back Keeps Me From Moving Into My Destiny

You can't help someone else if you can't help yourself.

Jesus said, "No man, having put his hand to the plow, and looking back, is fit for the kingdom of God" (Luke 9:62, KJV).

This scripture speaks volumes to me, and I feel it ties right into the act of forgiveness. Looking back keeps you from seeing what's in front of you and is a distraction to the destiny God planned for your life. Your destiny is not what happened to you, but it is the future you and I choose to live in. It is the *now*! By forgiving and letting go of my past, I am now able to heal. The healing process for me was when I chose to stop looking back. Gandhi once made a powerful statement that holds truth: "I will not let anyone walk through my mind with dirty feet" (M.K. Gandhi).

That is exactly what you do when you listen to the old voice of condemnation or the voice of your past. It is when you finally learn that a person's behavior has more to do with their internal struggle than it ever did with you that you learn GRACE! Then, it happens; one day, you wake up, and you're in this place where you're at peace with where you've been, at peace with what you've been through, and at peace with where you are going. Now, it's time to shake off the past! If we continue to live in yesterday (our past), we will never have the strength to live in victory (today). I used to like the idea of people thinking I had it all together. Now I can't wait to tell them how much of a mess I was and show them what the power of God can do. Remember that your past is what you have been through; it's not who you are. Start the process of forgiving by doing some forgiveness exercises. Sounds funny, I know, but just try it.

Forgiveness exercises are steps to forgive and empower your heart. Forgiveness exercises help you to let go of anger and release the burden of pain. Trust me, I had to put these exercises into motion in my life. The relief of forgiveness is resounding and unmistakable. At times it may come in small rushes, and at other times it comes in gentle waves bringing refreshment to your heart. Hurt is real, and as I stated before, holding onto hurt instead of healing can turn into resentment. Resentment fuels a grudge that often creates a wall around your heart. Make a choice. Be willing. Be open to letting go of grudges and resentments that have built up. This is a powerful step in forgiving.

Forgiveness is a complex act. The act of forgiving someone, whether they deserve it or not, calls upon the highest good or willingness that is within us. The actual act of forgiveness draws upon a place that is deep inside of you and me, where the highest of unconditional love exists. Forgiveness is for giving the pain a way out of your heart. Remember, letting go is not for the other person; it's for you! This process is so transforming and life-changing. By letting go, it allows your heart to experience relief and openness again. You're a fighter. Look at everything you've overcome. Don't give up now. I know this is a process, but it works if you are willing to let go and allow God to heal you. Again, it's not about the problem but the process.

I am not telling you to do something that I have not already done personally and am not still working on. I allowed unforgiveness to hold me back for almost three decades. For some, that's a lifetime! Don't keep looking back; this allows the hurt and pain of your past to keep you from your destiny. Just because we had a bad beginning chapter doesn't mean our ending chapter has to be bad. Our past is behind us, so let go and allow God to create the life He purposed for us! What God started in you, He is going to finish. Remember that you can't help someone else if you can't help yourself.

CHAPTER 7

There is a Story Behind My Praise!

"Know, first, who you are, and then adorn yourself
accordingly." (Epictetus)

Today as I begin this chapter, I pause and take a moment to look over my life, thanking God for His divine mercy and grace. "What, then, shall we say in response of these things? If God is for us, who can be against us?" (Romans 8:31 NIV) Allow God to heal you! The first steps are to own it (your pain) and then deal with it. If we never deal with our unresolved issues, they become who we are. We become broken, and often broken or hurt people hurt others. However, if you do not know you are broken, you may never know you are hurting other people. Your behavior becomes routine, and you will begin to tell yourself *this is who I am.*

Recognizing you are hurt and that you have been allowing your past to dictate your future will ultimately cause your healing process to activate, but you must first recognize it. Everything in life is a process. Look to God and be honest enough to say, Lord, I need You, and I can't do this without you. He already knows your pain. So, begin to move without hesitation into your God-given destiny. Choose to forgive in order to live your best life. God has blessed me with the most amazing husband of 35 years, who is the most loving father to our daughters and grandfather to our granddaughter. He has loved me through the good, the bad, and the ugly. He has been by my side when I was up and when I was down, even when I did not want to live. I was broken for a long time, but now I realize God placed him in my life so I could become whole. Believe me when I say it wasn't easy, but again, it is doable.

My faith in God and who He is has kept me. The question now is: why did it take so long? Why could I not move past my hurts and pains? Why did I allow my past to hold me hostage for decades? I (we) may never know the answer, and that's okay as long as we are unwilling to give up and sure to remember that the past could not have been any other way. While we may encounter some defeats in our lives, we must never allow ourselves to be defeated. My heart is grateful that God didn't give up on me. The undeniable fact is that what happened to me wasn't good, but it has worked for my good. The enemy is never after your history. He is always after your destiny. He is out to destroy everything you have been anointed and called to be from the time of birth. You and I have a choice; we can continue to hold on to the past and allow it to cripple us, or we can begin our healing process by allowing God to heal us.

We have to breathe and know this is just a chapter in our lives, not our whole story. We cannot continue our lives in bondage but rather recognize that everything we go through, we must grow through. No matter what we have been battling, God has a plan to bless us. Change will not come if we wait on someone to apologize. Don't let your past define you; leave it behind you. We were never created to live depressed, guilty, condemned, ashamed, or unworthy. We were created to be victorious. My hope now is to laugh as much as I have cried, to love, and have the courage to accept love in return. There is a story behind my praise.

CHAPTER 8

FREE to be ME

Once you fall in love with the process, results will follow.

Don't worry about who you were. For years I didn't think being me would be good enough. Go ahead and free yourself to be you. Unfortunately, holding on to resentment keeps you angry at the whole world. It causes you to walk around with the "why me" attitude. You never know how miserable you are until you become free. When we choose to heal, we begin to advocate for ourselves by truly understanding what we deserve. Healing is about leaving the effects of the past behind and focusing on what's now and what's best for you. According to God's Word in John 8:36: "Therefore if the Son makes you free, you shall be free indeed" (KJV).

Freedom is a wonderful thing. It is the ability to be who God created you to be: unapologetically YOU! You have to know who you are and whose you are. Even though my past has caused me pain, thank God it didn't kill me. If we never heal from our past hurts, we will always bleed on the people that didn't hurt us. I have been awed by letting go of my past, by truly forgiving.

Note to self: you can be healed and still healing.

For over 30 years, I carried that burden as if I were walking around bent over. What we focus on grows, whether good or bad. Now that I do not focus on the bad (past), I can walk straight up with my head held high. Again, I am not saying every day is a good day. I am saying that it is a choice, your choice, and no one else's.

You have to make a declaration daily to choose to be the best version of yourself and allow God to do the rest. Being free assures you that by allowing yourself to deal with your past and forgiving, you will be able to walk in your God-given destiny, your purpose. I am still learning each day to trust the process because now I know it was never about me. Again, I have had to learn to trust the process, and I am still learning. See, I realized I had to forgive to receive my healing. I didn't understand God's plan for my life. It was never about the problem but the process. As long as I allowed myself to keep looking back, I was never able to move forward. Once I fell in love with the process, I began to see the results. I understood my purpose.

In every part of our lives, we must know that God is still God. Never allow the silence of others to leave you questioning your worth. It's not up to others to direct your path, only God. Your comeback will be greater than your setback. It doesn't matter who you used to be or how you perceived yourself. All that matters is who you will become in the end. I have lived in mediocre land for far too long. So have you. So, let's not allow our past to control us anymore. Again, we can't let the ugly in others kill what God has placed on the inside of us. My mother is my mother; I have always loved her and always will. I now understand it was never about me but about a woman who never dealt with her unresolved issues. I pray that you heal over things no one ever apologized for. When you walk in your purpose, no one can take that from you. Own it. So, I encourage you to LIVE!

"Brethren, I count not myself to have apprehended: but this one thing I do, forgetting those things which are behind, and reaching forth unto those things which are before, I press toward the mark for the prize of the high calling of God in Christ Jesus" (Philippians 3:13-14, KJV). Therefore, I choose freedom! I am finally free to be me! You cannot move on until you accept these things, and you will certainly not receive closure in every situation, but you can create self-closure. Most of what others do is about them, not about you. Some people won't apologize because they can't. Some things can't be explained. While you cannot change other people, you can change yourself by allowing God's process to work in you.

Closure

After submitting my manuscript, the one thing that I needed full closure on came to light. Remember my story of me losing my baby girl at the age of 16. I've often wondered where she was buried as that was never disclosed to me. I thought I was okay with not knowing; however, I just couldn't seem to shake it. So reluctantly, with my counselor's advice, I decided to pursue the idea of trying to locate her grave. I want to add that my husband had wanted this for a long time. In my pursuit, I had no other choice but to ask my mother had my father said anything to her regarding the burial of my baby girl. However, just as I thought, she couldn't give me the answer I so desperately needed.

She did tell me of a person I could contact to get the answers I was looking for. Talk about healing!!! There was a time I would not have been able to ask my mother this because of fear. But God! I was able to reach out to the person she had mentioned. He was very helpful and sympathetic in listening to my request.

The first question was, "Do you have a death certificate"? No, I was only 16.

The second question, "Did you name the baby"? No, I was only 16.

I could sense his concern for this request. I began to cry as I explained the details surrounding the birth of my baby, and because of my age, I had no say in the matter. It sounds crazy, but it was my reality. So he assured me that he would do his best to look into the matter.

The next morning I received a call stating he had found the death certificate. Praise God, I thought to myself. The next step was to go to the courthouse to locate the burial plot. Two days had gone by, and no call until the third day. The phone rang, I answered, and there was a slight pause; my heart sank. He began the conversation with the words, "There is no record of burial." I thought to myself, "Why am I not surprised?" He goes on to tell me what he thought was a death certificate was just a form filled out and that the death was never sent to the state to be recorded. Okay, what was he trying to tell me? As gentle as he knew how he explained what happened. He said that what they (the funeral home and my dad) did was take my baby and just bury her. As horrible as that sounds, somewhere deep down, this is what I always dreaded would be the truth. This was what I had felt all these years.

Talk about a whirlwind. I thanked him for his time, and we hung up. For two days, I felt all the emotions of grief. Denial, anger, bargaining, depression, and acceptance. Denial, no way. Anger, how could he (my father)? Bargaining, well, maybe this wasn't the right information. I even tried to excuse my father. Depression, my father didn't think enough of me to do the right thing? And acceptance, this was who my father was (at that time). Wanting to stay in that place of pity, I remembered asking God to help me forgive my father for all the things he had or hadn't done. A little soft voice whispered, "ALL." I didn't realize this would happen almost four years after his death, but all meant ALL. August 7, 1982, the agony of losing her began. June 12, 2021, absolute closure. Evonna Shantae Dilworth-Portwine. She would have been 39 this year. Thank God for freedom.

A Letter to Felicia:

Felicia, the 18-year-old little girl. I release you to be the best you. You are no longer a part of who I am today. I choose Fe. I choose to be happy, healthy, and whole. No more looking back. The past is the past. I can't change the past, but I can change my future.

Eighteen-year-old Felicia, know it was not your fault, so you can let go of the guilt, the hurt, and the shame. You are finally free to be you. Choose to start living your best life, knowing it is not about the problem but the process. So again, I say to 18-year-old Felicia, "Goodbye." You have been a part of my life for too long, and your time is up. I am sorry for the things that happened to you: the hurt, the pain, the molestation, the losing of a baby, and so much more. The answer to the question of why is one you may never know. Felicia, I want you to know that you are beautiful, loved, smart, and worthy.

"I will praise thee; for I am fearfully and wonderfully made: marvelous are Thy works; and that my soul knoweth right well"
(Psalms 139:14, KJV).

References

"Issue." Merriam-Webster's Dictionary, Merriam-Webster. https://www.merriam-webster.com/dictionary/issue. Accessed 10 January 2021.

Stanley, A. (2012, April 17th). *How will we choose to view our hurts?* Retrieved October 10th, 2020, from https://ilifejourney.wordpress.com/tag/san-diego/

CPSIA information can be obtained
at www.ICGtesting.com
Printed in the USA
BVHW052025060921
616167BV00013B/261

9 781737 479130